I been there, so...

MERVYN MORRIS was born in Kingston, J~~~~~~~ at the University College of the West Indi~ at St Edmund Hall, Oxford. From 1966 staff of the University of the West Indies, ..~... ...~.. ..~ retired as Professor of Creative Writing and West Indian Literature. He has been a visiting Writer in Residence at the South Bank Centre in London, and undertaken readings and workshops in the Caribbean, Canada, the United States, England, Wales, Germany, Belgium and Malaysia. As editor, his books include Louise Bennett's *Selected Poems*, Michael Smith's *It A Come* and *The Faber Book of Contemporary Caribbean Short Stories*. Mervyn Morris is the author of *'Is English We Speaking' and other essays* (1999), incorporating the manuscript for which he won Jamaica's prestigious Una Marson Award in 1997, and *Making West Indian Literature* (2005), a collection of essays and interviews. His earlier collections of poetry include *The Pond* (1973, revised 1997), *Shadowboxing* (1979), *Examination Centre* (1992), *Vestiges* (published in a limited edition in 1996) and *On Holy Week* (1976, 1993). One of the Caribbean's most distinguished poets and critics, Mervyn Morris has been awarded the Institute of Jamaica's Centenary Medal and a Silver Musgrave Medal for poetry.

MERVYN MORRIS

I been there, sort of

NEW AND SELECTED POEMS

Emma & Josh,
with thanks
Mervyn Morris

CARCANET

First published in Great Britain in 2006 by
Carcanet Press Limited
Alliance House
Cross Street
Manchester M2 7AQ

Poems from *The Pond* (New Beacon Books 1973; revised edition 1997), *Shadowboxing* (New Beacon Books 1979) and *Examination Centre* (New Beacon Books 1992) reprinted by kind permission of New Beacon Books Ltd.

A CIP catalogue record for this book is available from the British Library
ISBN 1 85754 829 9
978 1 85754 829 7

The publisher acknowledges financial assistance from Arts Council England

Typeset by XL Publishing Services, Tiverton
Printed and bound in England by SRP Ltd, Exeter

for Helen

Acknowledgements

The author gratefully acknowledges the assistance of a Fulbright Fellowship to Lincoln University, Missouri, and a University of the West Indies Mona Campus Research Fellowship during which he worked on some of these poems.

Thanks also to *Aqueduct*, *Atlanta Review*, *Callaloo*, *The Caribbean Writer*, *The Jamaica Sunday Observer*, *Mississippi Review*, *Obsidian III*, *Pathways*, *Planet*, *Poetry International*, *Poetry Wales*, *Poui* and *World Literature Today*, in which some of the new poems appeared; and to Dangaroo Press (*On Holy Week*) and New Beacon Books (*The Pond*, *Shadowboxing* and *Examination Centre*).

Contents

I been there, sort of

On Holy Week

from *The Pond*

from *Shadowboxing*

from *Examination Centre*

Short Story

I

How carefully they walk
together, hardly ever touching.
Neither he nor she is rushing
into anything.

But something's going on
beneath the easy talk
of books & family & friends.
Read on.

II

They're in a private place
together, searching
through the story, getting to know
the characters, intertwining
themes, discretion & desire,
exploring conflict, complication,
restructuring lives
in the imagination.

III

Goodbye. 'Let's keep in touch,'
they say, without conviction.
They hug each other warmly, and depart.
But each has nestled in the other's art,
so it's another story in the fiction.

Critic

Questions about meaning
really concern you now
whose deconstruction, exquisite
unravelling, terrorised.
You were in control.

Did you misread her eyes
when, leafing through a magazine
in bed, she glanced your way?

Unstable text, your wife
has broken up the game.
Now she has left you, academic
reading doesn't seem the same.

Dialogue for One

for the NDTC

in this
reflective
exercise

the bodies
imitate

contraction
and release

each
glistening

performing
mirror

honouring
the other

artfully
dancing
identity

At a Poetry Reading

Negotiating strangers
and inscrutable desires,
the old pretenders hope to be
accepted as constructive liars.

If, playing parts, they can avoid the spurious
(the false pretence, the histrionic fraud)
and manage the occasional epiphany,
some of the other actors will applaud.

Behind the Curtain

Behind the curtain, when we knew
the audience hadn't come,
the ugly mood of histrionic sorrow
was broken by an actor playing dumb
patrician: 'Will the damn fools come tomorrow?'

Encounter

When I was stumbling
in the dark, confused
and crying out for help,
this friendly fellow seemed amused;

and while I fought like anything
to keep the candle lit
he cheerfully reviewed
the guttering of my wit.

Astonished that the brother found
my struggle such a treat
I turned the flickering light on him
and glimpsed his cloven feet.

Proposition One

A routine love that hangs its hat
on coming home and wipes its feet
precisely every afternoon, and greets
its wife with proper peck and asks
how went the day, is not for me.
Love will not set the clock
by my affections
and wind its own springs up
in time.

To keep the thing alive
let's loosen up,
let's improvise, my love,
relax, be casual, enjoy the lime,
relinquish the habitual,
reshape the paradigm.

The Pledge

I

She's black
and beautiful
you lucky nigger
poet sing

II

I love her
black I love
her sensual
grace

I love her
black I love
her bright
enquiring face

digging truth
beyond my eyes
weeding dark lies

I love her black

III

but she says No
Stay with me nigger
lover keep it true
Say with me nigger

I love her
   (love her)
Also we are black
      (are black)
      (are black)

Autograph Album

That boy who loved you
(and you loved him but never told him so)
has scrawled his epitaph on your pink vellum.

The girl whom you detested (and who knew)
has paid you back – with troubling ambiguity,
neatly on the back side of your best friend's
witty retching.

The lad you asked just to be kind
has pulled a big surprise, has written
something shrewd yet generous to a fault.

This album
is a minefield floating,
waiting to sink your craft.

Reunion

long long ago
we heard the eyes
vote *no*

not here
not yet
not ever

but the whirligig
of time
has brought us round

years after
that brief pantomime

and we are playing
new games now

acknowledging the strain
of lust inside our laughter

Tournament

Nostalgic devils 'playing for fun'
in their declining years,
they scramble till the match is done
and smile as if to say, 'Who cares?'

That loser, sweltering
in bed, contending with a sheet,
he cares. He's grappling
with midnight memories of defeat.

Birthdays

The game is metaphor.
'Birthdays: reassuring corners
in the long, dark room of time.'

'Reminder knots,' another voice
proposes. 'Birthdays are reminders
time is heartless, beauty fades.'

There is no string of time
unravelling till the end is cut,
only a dark pool swirling –
letters, matches, galliwasps,
toothpaste tubes and railway tickets,
myriad markers from our lives
in seminal confusion, falsified
by cuckoo-clocks and calendars.

I, celebrating birthdays
in the whirlpool, dream:
something will grow in time.

Eve

the garden
seemed

a proper
paradise

until
she buck up

on a serpent
talking nice

Connection

Discombobulated
by his riddling eyes,
the foxy lady tries
to seem untouched, but may
have seriously miscalculated.
The predator can sense
her willingness to end her
laughable pretence.
She wants to play
surrender.

Parlour Game

Antennae register
enticement, picking up
glances and the enigmatic
smile.

Superfly is tripping
into trouble, visioning
himself entangled
in her script.

Operation

after a thorough
physical

he dug a hole
into her skull

he cut
a great big window
in her gut

then mumbling how
he was so sorry but
he couldn't stay

the fucker
walked away

Happy Hour

her laughter quivers
like a flimsy bridge
before it breaks

her laughter covers up
a hole
and sharpened stakes

but the detested animal
is potent still it seems

the prepossessing monster
dominates her dreams

Pantomime

She smiled and smiled and seemed to be
the genial friend, the keen collaborator
until the transformation scene; then she
became a block of stone, a champion hater.

Moment of Truth

as both were
always listening
for what was being said
inside civilities

the genial courtesies
did not drown out
their body language
whispering exchange

and they maintained the dialogue
sotto voce many months
until the clash of glances
the electrifying flash

Interview

He sits there
looking thoughtful
slyly
taking me in

from top to bottom
eyes / bust / legs

meandering
through the detail
of my life & times
simpatico

but i can feel
the charge
that he does not
acknowledge

i know he knows i see
the amber light

& will not cross
the bridge

Persephone

i sleep & wake
& see the dream again –

the spectre
of my youthful paramour

my profiling adonis
begging to be gored

my faithless lover cruising
at the cemetery gate

Casanova

Flaunting his gym-toned pectorals,
washboard stomach, fashion-
conscious locks, he worked the image
of philanderer, every woman's
fantasy or threat.

But something tremulous inside
his gravelly baritone exposed
a small boy quivering in the dark,
his mother dead, his father gone away,
groping for explanations.

North Coast Hotel

the lovely pregnant lady
leaning on the disco bar
lets dancehall flow
through her

an elegant
black patrician
breaking out

before her man
a chunky brother
decorously sipping wine

while she is moving
like a native to the bass
teaching the child
dancehall

Cabal

Dem beg him, beg him, till dem sick
an tired – him wouldn sign him name
to what de most a dem waan lick
de opposition with. Him seh, 'Same

knife stick sheep stick goat,' an walk
out of de room. De big-man bus
a funny laugh. Nobody never talk
to him like dat. Him seh, 'Trust

me, eediot mus learn.' So, first of all,
we kick de eediot out de group. An den
we start de rumour seh him bawl
fi mercy when we check de books again –

yuh never know him tief? Yes, man, tief
like puss, unless yuh watchin him! An now
dat him expose, pure grief
to get another job. Him shoulda bow!

Me scratch your back, you scratch mine;
but if yuh tun traitor yuh must pay.
Dyamn fool! De eediot bwoy was tryin
to block de road. We move him out de way.

A Poet of the People

The pressure of the public made it smart
to turn away from 'self-indulgent Art'.
He found immediate applause inviting,
and gave himself wholeheartedly to writing
poems for the people, loud and clear.

When people didn't seem to care
much whether he wrote well or not –
how was nothing, everything was what –
he changed his mind again. And so,
thinking to have another go
at 'self-indulgent Art', he turned
towards the woman he had spurned,
his ever-loving personal Muse,
believing she could not refuse
him. But she did. She left him there,
writing for the people, loud and clear.

november sunlight
climbing up the shoulders of
the simmering poets

Advisory

They praise you for commitment,
your positive approach
to the whole heap o' problems
people broach.

Have fun being chatted-up,
but don't buy in–
to any sweet-mouth programme.
Do your own thing.

Remind them you're committed
to the line
that saying what you feel
is fine,

positive or negative
or in-between.
Don't let anybody
lock you in.

Montage

England, autumn, dusk —
so different from that quarter-hour
at home when darkness drops:
there's no flamboyant fireball
laughing a promise to return;
only a muted, lingering farewell,
and day has passed to evening.

Post-colonial Identity

The language they're conducted in
dictates the play in these debates.
Good english, as they say, discriminates.
White people language white as sin.

Peelin Orange

Dem use to seh
yu peel a orange
perfec
an yu get new clothes

But when mi father try
fi teach mi
slide de knife
up to de safeguard thumb

I move de weapon like
a saw inna mi han
an de dyamn rind
break

An if yu have de time
yu can come see mi
in mi ole clothes
peelin

Oblation

Then shall the poet say:

Draw near, and touch
my suppurating wounds.

This is my psyche
broken for you. Give thanks.

You have not cared enough.
But you may clap.

Toasting a Muse

One man who came to dinner
wouldn't eat,
just focused on his hostess
instant eloquent devotion.
He'd stand and say, as if proposing
a toast, 'I speak this in your honour,
ma'am, you are so beautiful,'
then chant some passionate verse,
and sit and drink some more
until the spirit moved in him
again, then stand and say
'You are so beautiful' et cetera
and do another item.
Funny fellow. Poet. Mad as hell.

I been there, sort of.
For in that ambience I too
was smitten, by what seemed
to me unusual radiance,
beauty of spirit lighting up the place,
but I kept quiet about it, made small talk,
stayed sober, and enjoyed the food.

Heritage

whispering ancestors
enfold me in their loving
ghostly immanence

Muntu

for Janheinz Jahn

My ancestors
alive inside the daylight
closed up invisible in air
float from the pages of your book.
We called their names.

Enter my father, laughing,
a substantial black.
(When I was young he died.)
Behind him his black father,
formidable, stern.
Fathers who fathered me.

My mother's mother shuffles in,
dragging her gentleness along the glare.
She indicates her father,
who looks white.
I start to hear the irons clink.
He dissipates my terror with a wink.

Sentences for Heritage Week

Mine history
for the energy it frees.

Do not spend precious time
hanging from family trees.

Having Eyes that See

The blind man led by a little boy
goes tap–tap–tapping down the street,
and foolishly I feel accused
for having eyes that see.

That blind man at the bus stop regularly
feeling along the window's edge –
'Thanks, God bless you,' shuffling on –
breeds like a chigger in my mind.

And leafing through a magazine
I am confronted by an ad,
'Tell me, what colour is the wind?'

I shan't let spurious guilt
take hold and steer me
into gloom, and yet
I think I see
a shadowy connection.

Thank-you Note

first you say
i mustnt write a
routine letter

then photographs
arrive
& photocopies

& you say
tomorrow
tomorrow
i shall write

& then in time you
dont know how
to say i should have
written you before but
this is just to say

Gaffes

We try to smother
troublesome remarks,
but hurtful truths
(however casual) survive,
fluttering tenaciously,
defiantly alive.

Boarding School

Saturday is pictures evening,
chairs are carried to the gym;
happy little boys enquire
'Who is in it?' 'What's the flim?'
'What's the flim? And who is in it?
Rita Hayworth? Doris Day?'
With a whirr the old projector
wafts excited boys away.

Do not let that tricky bastard
touch your treasure, you damn fool!
Spurn the dawg! Humiliate him!
Tie a tin can to his tool!
Come with me instead, I beg you;
trust me, I will treat you right.
Sexy-body, Nice-gal, Sweetness,
climb the stairs with me tonight.

Sunday morning: to the chapel
after breakfast off we go,
dressed to kill in suit and tie
(we're extras in the Sunday show),
to pray and otherwise perform
as reverential prodigies,
sing the hymns and look fulfilled,
no matter what the message is.

Can the preacher counteract
the awesome power of Hollywood?
Has he seen Delilah dancing?
Does he know her legs are good?
Who's he talking to, I wonder.
Does he know the flesh is sweet?
Does he know that wine's for drinking?
Does he know that bread's to eat?

Caning

Bend, boy, bend: *a dog's*
obey'd in office. Bend.
Empty your pockets, please,
and touch your toes.

I am the system, boy: authority:
the master, guardian of roles.
Behave, or suffer.
Bend now, bend.

Other routines obscure
this fundamental.
Prayers, classes,
lunchtime, tea,
house matches, prep,
a beer, an argument
about the team,
the piles of books
we have to mark,
distract us from the stark
brutality of our regime.
Robes and furr'd gowns hide all.

After the Movie

So they all had tea on the ceiling,
                        floating,
high on laughs!

But Mary Poppins flew away,
and the little boy wept in the dark.

Dragged into daylight he is weeping still.

Tutorial

'I'm strange,'
you said,
like an apology
with just a hint
of cool defiance.

But you are not
alone, remember;
it is strange inside
the labyrinthine
network wiring
each and every
head, a mess
of shimmering
mirrors,
a surreal forest
of reflection.
You may not
be as different
as you think.

Enjoy, examine
what you find.

Welcome
to the mystery
of mind.

Asylum

I

a fellow in the madhouse cries
the world is wallowing in lies
innocence is nevermore
the fat worm nestles at the core

II

Fix what you can. Forget the rest.
A little learnt indifference is best.

To Tell the Truth

i used to burn my poems
he said

was troubled
murmuring inside

till puking demons
brought relief

but no one
ever analysed

or even
saw

the stuff
i vomited

i used to burn my poems

Counsellor

Reaching out
with irony

she greets
our tensions

registers the timbre
of our screams

Critique

Yuh a grow, yuh wi come si
            Jamaican proverb

Authenticity for you
is blazing revelation,
the suicidal nerve
exposed, the madman
naked in the street.

One day, one day,
if you live long enough,
you'll feel the fire
in sobriety, give thanks
for smouldering restraint.

Anniversary Proceedings

Clinton and Barbara,
you stand accused
of Christian practices,
of faith in God and helpfulness
to people. You habitually buoy
us up with cheerfulness, which is
the very heart of your offence:
your challenge to a world of friction,
the marvel of your unaffected joy.

In view of all the evidence,
we vote for your conviction.

Clinton and Barbara,
you shall serve hereafter
another forty years
of love and laughter.

Granny

When Granny died
I stumbled in and out
her place, remembering
banana porridge, fumbling
her dog-eared bible,
faded bedspread,
musty cushions, hugging
memories of her love.

From the overflowing funeral
this fingled programme
is a talisman I carry
everywhere. Love is with me still.

Praise the Lord

full tabernacle
shouting to the shimmy of
wicked tambourines

At Church

the old man
stumbles in
a grisly sermon
DEATH
THE ULTIMATE
EXAM   stop writing   time

beyond him
stained glass
morning sun
the risen christ
and two or three
apostles

Diptych

I

when the wild guitarist
making too much noise
was thrown out by
his friend
he hanged himself

the day the music stopped
i came by
& was blasted
by the poui tree's
golden indifference

II

when the drunken painter
messing up the place
was thrown out by
the woman paying the rent
he hanged himself

& when he died
she gave away his last
pathetic canvases
of sombre figures
& the poui weeping gold

Au Revoir

He loved her madly,
cherishing her witty candour,
raunchy jokes,
tenacious *joie de vivre*.

After she left him for a nursing home,
each evening at their silent bungalow
the table would be set for two
and he would dine alone.

Last week Thursday, on his birthday,
after a whisky in the fading light,
he heard her breathe, 'Enough'.
He wiped his eyes and, like a courtier,
bowed low to kiss her shrivelled hand.

Farewell Function

he basked in admiration
dreaming
paradise

until
his metamorphosis

into a morbid
out-of-body witness
at the operation

like a patient etherised
returning
from the edge

& catching an obituary
draught

Transitions

for Alli & Joyce

In church triumphant
only months ago
he gave away the prize

but now at Eastertide
the father of the bride
is dead

bequeathing us
perpetual open house
a family of friends

and urging that we rise
above our sorrows
and terrestrial ends

Garden

after a shower
blackbirds preening on the grass
dressing for heaven

Postcard

from Longarone

Green fields
a vineyard
red–roofed cottages
a farmer & his dog
before the flood

& here
at panel two
grey miles of waste
a desolating tract

What countervailing
message
do you scrawl
on this

this glossy *memento
mori*

Epitaph

for Nita Barrow, 1916–1995

A very special human being,
genial, compassionate and wise,
she helped us see what she was seeing,
our true potential playing in her eyes.

Jamaican Dance #2

for Oswald Russell

Bereavement singing
from the instrument,
interrogating death,
the nine-night
in your left hand
wringing grief.

Birds twittering
their fore-day call
and response.
Sammy dead-oh,
Sammy dead-oh.
Bawl, woman, bawl.

A Chant Against Death

for Aidan & Ruth

          say family
                          say friends
say wife
   say love
              say life

say learning
                    laughter
            sunlight
                           rain

    say cycle
                    circle
   music
              memory

say night & day
        say sun & moon

      say
  see you soon

A Word

please to
burn the body
when i die
& scatter
ashes in the wind

so there is nothing
physical to focus on
when i am gone

& please to
let me linger
in the memory of a few
close friends & family
a month or two

On Holy Week

a sequence of poems for radio

Prologue by the Maker

Beware: the following secular depiction
of people living through the Crucifixion
revises Holy Writ. The gospel story triggers
the maker's thinking about various figures:
he offers moments, voices, attitudes;
and if, occasionally, faith intrudes
don't blame the maker, blame the borrowed bible
(for humanist agnostics, unreliable).

The maker who presents these versions
is grateful, in advance, to all those persons
(including the Almighty) who'll forgive him
his ordinary rhyme and rhythm,
allow each portrait arguably true,
and kindly authorise invention too.

Now hear these people. Some are good.
Some fail to do the things they should;
but hear them all. Let each one speak
a little of Unholy Week.

Jesus in Gethsemane

I

O Father − if it be thy will −
let this cup pass from me.
But O my Father, I submit to thee:
use me, thy servant, still.

II

Father, I cannot drink this cup!
Release me (if it be thy will).
Unwilling, Father, I am still
thy servant. Bear me up.

A Priest

The chap's a madman rather than a liar:
I think he's quite convinced he's the Messiah!
That God might be a carpenter! Absurd!
It's quite the silliest nonsense I have heard!
(You know my bias; but) a priest –
perhaps an elder, at the very least –
would seem to be more likely for the job
than some untutored Galilean yob!

Judas

That evening, not so long ago,
the Master, fingers in the dish,
said gently: 'Did I not choose
you twelve, yet one of you's
a devil?' Mocking, he glanced
at me; and others, quick
on cue, looked my way too.
The odd man out is always
Judas. 'We're from Galilee.'
(Nasty little province,
smells of fish!)

The point is,
Jesus never trusted me.
John, who's favourite, he's
from Galilee. Like Peter,
Andrew, all the cosy band.
Which Galilean, Lord,
will sit at your right hand?

Tonight I kissed him
and I saw
that mocking glance again.
'Betrayest thou the Master

with a kiss?' he said, ironic; then
seemed pleased or something
like relieved he'd got me
right. That knowing judge of men,
he surely ought to realise
that truths are often complicated:
what he spotted he created,
distrusting with those distant
foreign eyes.

The point is not the money, I'll
go give it back. For, hell,
what's thirty bits of silver?
I would not sell
the Master, he's for free. Just
preserve my purity of hate
for him I served and loved so well.
My Lord, the Master of my fate,
always withheld his trust.

Pilate's Wife

I dreamt us strolling, arm in loving arm,
along the avenue that skirts the border;
our tender courting days wheeled back.
Just then we heard a yapping,
loud, a pack in full pursuit!

Into our lives he crashed,
a lamb, bleeding and bruised,
and weary with the chase.
I picked him up and cuddled him
in my warm arms, my newest baby boy.

The hounds were yelping louder,
nuzzling the hedge. And then
(but why? but why?) you snatched
the poor thing from my arms,

and with 'We must not interfere,
my love, the dogs demand their prey,'
you tossed their quarry over
the prickly hedge. The ravenous pack
were through him in an instant,
ravaging the body.

That moment, in my dream,
our sweet love died; that afternoon
I sat alone, playing with thorns.
At length, I turned to you
to plead forgiveness.
You offered that, and love;
but, broken in simple grief,
I could not take your proffered
bread and wine.

Pilate

And then I tried to pass the buck;
but Herod, with astute aplomb,
politely, sent him back.

I tried to move the people
to accept he might be freed
this feast of the Passover.
'Kill him! Kill him! Nail him
to the cross!' They clamoured for
Barabbas, insurrectionist, a bandit
who's attacked imperial rule.
'Try Jesus for yourselves,' I told the mob;
'You judge him by your law.'
'Kill him!' they hollered louder,
'Nail him to the cross!'

Then slimy priests, those holy rogues
of politics, began to turn the screws:
'You must not fail to sentence Christ,

soi-disant King of Jews.
Your masters wouldn't like it much
if we should let them know
we caught a man supplanting Rome
and you have let him go.'

My basic job is keeping peace
and reverence for Rome. The man
was bad for both. I had to yield.
'I find no fault in him,' I cried,
and ordered water brought;
and, public gesture of defeat
(sound politics, I thought),
I washed these loving
histrionic hands.
The crowd surprised me, seized
the guilt of their demands.

    You know
I am not weak. I could, I would
stand up for Jesus if I thought
that were the thing to do. Now
he is dead. He didn't seem to care,
so why should you? How is your head,
my sweet?

Peter

O Jesus, you were right:
I have denied you, Lord; in spite
of protestation, failed
the test.

      When that girl hailed
Me, Lord, I should have hollered loud,
'He's God I follow!', Lord, and faced the crowd.
For all my talk, somehow
I couldn't then; it's too late now:
the deed is done, and twice the cock has crowed.
O Lord, more than this worthless life I owed
to you who made the world make sense!

Though hard on overconfidence,
you taught that fear is lack of faith, is sin;
yet I denied you, Lord, to save my skin.
These bitter tears won't wash away the stain.

But O my Jesus, let me try again:
make me, as promised, your foundation rock;
forgive me, Lord, and I will feed your flock.

Soldiers

Hey! Boy! If you are God
then say who spit on you!
Say who, you bloody fraud!

We're gonna nail you, Lord!

Simon of Cyrene

Why me? It's
just my luck.
Another great
procession
coming through,
some carpenter
called Christ.
Women weeping,
people jeering,
and the Roman
soldiers hard
and cold, 'Hey, you!'
Not me? 'Hey! You!'
I didn't figure.
'Take this cross!'
Orders is orders
from a Roman guard.
I'm strong enough,
and this man Christ
is weary, bleeding,
scourged so deep.

Wicked heavy
plank of wood,
the cross I bore
for Jesus. 'King
of Jews' the sign said.
Rubbish. Wonder what
he'd done?

A Woman Named Mary

We get a good view here.

I know that man.
It's Jesus! I've anointed him –
in Bethany, I think: at Simon's house.
A lovely piece of man; real sweet.
Those hands. That mouth. Those feet.
Some stingy bastard tried to say
the money spent on nard was waste,
and should have gone to help the poor!
Jesus spoke up for me.

Jesus on the Road

Weep not for me but for yourselves
and all the world to come. For some
shall bless their barren luck
that they have never given suck;
and they shall pray the mountain fall
and hide them from the sky.
Such evil, and the tree is green;
much more when it is dry.

Malefactor (Left)

So you is God?
Den teck wi down! Tiefin doan bad
like crucifyin!
Wha do you, man?
Save all a wi from dyin!

Malefactor (Right)

Doan bodder widdim, Master; him
must die;
but when you kingdom come, remember I.
When you sail across de sea,
O God of Judah, carry I wit dee.

Centurion

I've seen it often:
when the pain gets harsh,
the fellow up there on the cross
will often cry for mercy. Usually
if he is lucid he will curse.
Sometimes when the pain gets harsh
the victim stops proclaiming
he is innocent,
and swears revenge.
But this man's different: he forgave
the people who enjoyed his pain!
Never nailed a man like this before.
Surely this man was God.

Mary (Mother)

To see him
strung up there
between two robbers,
scorned, abused!

I still remember when
an angel, as they say,
predicted him;
and Joseph; and those
tough uncomfortable
miles to Bethlehem;
and bedding in a stable,
for the inn was full;
and giving birth.

O God, the pain!
To hear him cry! To see
the head fall slack!
The wounded hands! The spear–slit
in his side!

John

I fished; but he was deep.
The perfect man. Divine.
His love
was everlastingly benign.

Stripped there,
broken on the cross:
perfection sacrificed!
O help us to endure our loss,
blessed body of Christ.

Joseph of Arimathaea

Sometimes, avoiding trouble, we accept defeat.
(Painful sometimes, being discreet.)

Soon Sabbath now. The corpse of Christ
ought to come down by then.
Which means pulling strings again.
I think I'll bury him where I
had planned to have my own bones lie.

Thank God there's something I can do.
Forgive me, Lord, for not proclaiming you.

Mary Magdalene

Me, crying; just outside the tomb.
This fellow asks me why I'm crying.
I ask him where the body is.
'Mary,' the man says quietly.

I turn.
                    The voice is His.

Thomas

Sure, I'm lacking faith. It's just
I am not gullible like some.
Better to be wrong than dumb.

There is no doubt
I loved the King of Men.
But if he seem to come again
some simple test must be applied:
I'll plunge these fingers in his riven side
to know, first-hand, that what I see
is him that died.

Doubt's my creed:
till time breeds proof
sand seems more honest than rock.
If my Lord lives, he'll meet the need
of those who question, those who mock;
of us who, wanting faith, will stand aloof.

from The Pond

Valley Prince

for Don Drummond, 1943–1969

Me one, way out in the crowd,
I blow the sounds, the pain,
but not a soul
would come inside my world
or tell mi how it true.
I love a melancholy baby,
sweet, with fire in her belly;
and like a spite
the woman turn a whore.
Cool and smooth around the beat
she wake the note inside mi
and I blow mi mind.

Inside here, me one
in the crowd again,
and plenty people
want mi blow it straight.
But straight is not the way; my world
don' go so; that is lie.
Oonoo gi mi back mi trombone, man:
is time to blow mi mind.

Stripper

At a sleazy club where strippers are on view
a weary poet stopped for wine
and song; but had to take the stripper too,
whose writhing seemed an image of his line.
She put on clothes to take them off, she wore
performing pieces, such a fuss she made
of skimpy little veils before
her parts (which never were displayed)!
Riddling hard to music, she performed
her teasing art, for which the patron paid.
Nice fleshy legs, gyrating hips that warmed
the watchers; sensuous, lively, educated tits.
The poet looked away, to check the eyes
of grim-faced lechers, soft men going to bits,
suckers deceived by lighting, sold on lies
(while there behind the smoke-dimmed crowd
the cunning pander lurked, a ponce on guard).
She took the last piece off the law allowed.
The poet felt his symbol growing hard.

To an Expatriate Friend

Colour meant nothing. Anyone
who wanted help, had humour or was kind
was brother to you; categories of skin
were foreign; you were colour-blind.

And then the revolution. Black
and loud the horns of anger blew
against the long oppression; sufferers
cast off the precious values of the few.

New powers re-enslaved us all:
each person manacled in skin, in race.
You could not wear your paid-up dues;
the keen discriminators typed your face.

The future darkening, you thought it time
to say goodbye. It may be you were right.
It hurt to see you go; but, more,
it hurt to see you slowly going white.

To the Unknown Non-combatant

When the battle started
he was quick to duck.
He lay on his face in the open street
cursing his luck.

'Come join us!' (voices from the left).
'Come help us in the fight!'
'Be honest with yourself; you're ours,'
said voices from the right.

Meanwhile the bullets overhead
were troubling him somewhat
and buildings burning either side
had made the middle hot.

He thought perhaps he'd better choose.
He crawled to join a side.
A bullet clapped him in the neck –
of course he died.

They left him face-down in the dust,
carcass going rotten.
Bullets whistled overhead.
He was forgotten.

The Day My Father Died

The day my father died
I could not cry;
My mother cried,
Not I.

His face on the pillow
In the dim light
Wrote mourning to me,
Black and white.

We saw him struggle,
Stiffen, relax;
The face fell empty,
Dead as wax.

I'd read of death
But never seen.
My father's face, I swear,
Was not serene.

Topple that lie,
However appealing:
That face was absence
Of all feeling.

My mother's tears were my tears,
Each sob shook me:
The pain of death is living,
The dead are free.

For me my father's death
Was mother's sorrow;
That day was her day,
Loss was tomorrow.

Outing

A rush of boys reporting in.
Enquiry, and a hush.

'Drowned, drowned, Marriott is drowned.'

That curious thirst for detail swells;
in waves the teachers rise
like undertakers
and descend the cold stone steps.

Little Boy Crying

Your mouth contorting in brief spite and hurt,
your laughter metamorphosed into howls,
your frame so recently relaxed now tight
with three-year-old frustration, your bright eyes
swimming tears, splashing your bare feet,
you stand there angling for a moment's hint
of guilt or sorrow for the quick slap struck.

The ogre towers above you, that grim giant,
empty of feeling, a colossal cruel,
soon victim of the tale's conclusion, dead
at last. You hate him, you imagine
chopping clean the tree he's scrambling down
or plotting deeper pits to trap him in.

You cannot understand, not yet,
the hurt your easy tears can scald him with,
nor guess the wavering hidden behind that mask.
This fierce man longs to lift you, curb your sadness
with piggy-back or bull-fight, anything,
but dare not ruin the lessons you should learn.

You must not make a plaything of the rain.

Shadows

When the man taps out
a peephole in his crown,
that hole into the dark
pit is for peering down:
but it is hard to tell
what's going on down there:
when shadows thrash
and slither
what we glimpse
are figures either
wrestling for fun or
locked in combat
in a subterranean war.

The Roaches

We had a home. The roaches came
to stay. They spread until they had control
of kitchen, pantry, study, then the whole
damned house. We fought them, but the game
was set. We sprayed, and they kept breeding all the same.

We found a house with plenty space,
clean and dry and full of light.
We checked beneath the sink – no roach in sight.
We checked the cupboards – not a trace
of roaches. No roach anyplace.

And so we moved.
                          The roaches came.
We sprayed, but they kept breeding all the same.

The Pond

There was this pond in the village
and little boys, he heard till he was sick,
were not allowed too near.
Unfathomable pool, they said,
that swallowed men and animals just so;
and in its depths, old people said,
swam galliwasps and nameless horrors;
bright boys kept away.

Though drawn so hard by prohibitions,
the small boy, fixed in fear, kept off;
till one wet summer, grass growing lush,
paths muddy, slippery, he found himself
there at the fabled edge.

The brooding pond was dark.
Sudden, escaping cloud, the sun
came bright; and, shimmering in guilt,
he saw his own face peering from the pool.

Narcissus

They're lying; lying, all of them:
he never loved his shadow.
He saw it was another self
and tried to wring its neck.
Not love but murder on his mind,
he grappled with the other man
inside the lucid stream.

Only the surface broke.
Unblinking eyes
came swimming back in view.

At last he knew
he never would
destroy that other self.
And knowing made him shrink.

He shrank into a yellow-bellied flower.

Mariners

who are
the night-cruisers
slicing through dark
dim on the foredeck
scanning for shark

we are
the seafarers
sick in the deep
bilious in daylight
troubled asleep

we are the sea-searchers
scaling the night
keen in the darkness
fish-eyed in light

from Shadowboxing

Muse

When you woo her
she will fade

This is how
the game is played

    Smilingly
    she leads him on
    He approaches
    Whereupon

    the figure in the
    evening air
    begins to
    slowly disappear

Extraordinary
trade
When you woo her
she will fade

This is how
the game is played

Afro-Saxon

I

Another friend arraigns me:
too detached, he says,
absurdly free
of all the ways of feeling
true blacks, as a rule,
now share: Be funky, brother,
or be cool!

Okay. Though blackness isn't new
to me: ten, fifteen years ago
I didn't need
a uniform, my skin would do:
but I am learning, brother;
I'll succeed...

II

He never made it. Thought-
inspectors, quivering at the sight
of an Afro-Saxon on the road
towards the border, caught
him sneaking in-
to Blackness, radioed:
Don't let that nigger fool you, he is White!

For Consciousness

Ol' plantation wither,
factory close down,
brothers of de country
raisin' Cain in town.

An' now dem in de city
sweatin' blood dem fin'
is jus' like de same system
dem mean to lef' behin':

but agents of de owners–dem
is harder now to sight –
plenty busha doan ride horse
an' some doan t'ink dem white.

In de new plantation story
firs' t'ing dat have to know
is who an' who to tackle
when de call to battle blow.

Cave

but further in
a lightbeam
spotted clothing
on the ground
a shirt
that smelt of the man

tracking
along close passages
they picked up
shoes and socks
a vest
his trousers
finally a brief
reminder
smelling of the crutch

and then at last
in a little room
like a cell
at the centre

they found him
huddled naked
in the dark

A Voyage

'Beware, beware their evil song:
they eat your flesh,
they bleach your bones,
you won't last long.'

His vessel neared an island.
Shimmering calm. Air still.
Enthralling song
across the green sea floating

paralysed his will.

O heaven within his reach,
he felt. And swam for shore.

His fortune waited, lolling on the beach.

Meeting

I

An unfamiliar bed
of radicals. And me
looking to root
out lies.

A nightmare –
comrade after comrade
springing
up to criticise!

I took
to planting
questions
in your eyes.

II

spuriously dry
we banter
knowing

something
critical
is growing
underground

a movement
threatening
solidarity

In the Garden

Until the fascinating snake
she didn't know, she didn't want to know.

But when the serpent, tired of being eyed,
unwreathed himself to go,
Eve yielded. 'No,' she cried,
'I'll have a taste.' And so…

Togetherness

If ever two were one, then surely we.
Anne Bradstreet

I

Lying in the dark together
we
in wordless dialogue
defined community.

II

You switch the light on to inspect
an alien remark.
And now your body stutters.

No more lying in the dark.

Dreamtime

the lady dreams
herself shut out
her lord in the castle
his lady without

he waves from a window
a long way away
she doesn't know what
he intends to convey

one evening in dreamtime
the wind blew right
and a voice floated down
from that worrying height

i live in a castle
with very thick walls
and the drawbridge drawn
up tight

A Birthday Poem

Peel-head john-crow circling

year after year habitually conveys
congratulations dead on time;

each year it wheezes, hovering:
'Happy birthday: you decline

hereafter, everything decays.'
Supernal mockery presents

that gliding messenger on time
each year, in pantomime

of blessing, wry malevolence
of joy before our wasting innocence.

Terminal

She's withering
before our eyes

and no one
noticeably

cries
We do

the hopeful
ritual

each day
we bring

fresh fruit
we prattle

and we pray
for hours

Her room
is heavy

with the scent
of flowers

Checking Out

I slam the door. 'Dear, are you positive
there's nothing left?' Well, no:
something remains, I'm sure of that:

some vestige of our lives in this bare flat
will linger, some impulse will outlive
our going, recycled in the flow

of being. We never leave,
we always have to go.

from Examination Centre

Examination Centre

Dilapidated room,
paint peeling.
Sufferers
on edge.

The chief invigilator
gives the word.
The fingered papers rustle.

Outside the centre –
part of my recall –
trees bend and stretch
and breathe.
Winds, playful, tease.

We're struggling here
with questions
and time
and longing
for a life we glimpse
through dust
clouding the panes.

Love Is

a giving
& a measured taking

amputation
re-creating

everlasting
interface

a prison
& an open space

a teasing glimpse
of holy grail

a generator
that can fail

the naked jugular
the knife

the torsion
balance in my life

Peacetime

bomb-disposal
combed the area
& declared it clean

but love i cannot
guarantee
safe conduct

through the rubble
of my dreams —

i've read
too many people
blown to bits

by landmines
lying silent
in the dust

long after
all those bells
& all that joy

long after solemn treaties
had been signed & sealed

Sister

beneath the undulating
calm
dark currents move

recalling
hurt & rage
& fracture

o my romantic soul
sister longing
for a whole

new world of love
i hear your soft song
breaking on the page

Seen

beyond the longing
& the lies

half-hidden in
equivocating eyes

(be careful
if you can't be good)

a lurking dread
of being

understood

There Was a Young Poet

There was a young poet
who thrived on his pain
(Hey ho the sun and the rain)
His woman ran off
and he found her again
(Hey ho the sun and the rain)

It pleased him to ask for
a foot in the face
(Hey ho the sun and the rain)
Whenever it hurt enough
words fell in place
(with a Hey ho the sun and the rain)

It happened one summer
nobody knows why
(Hey ho the sun and the rain)
  The woman he said he loved
  happened to die
(Hey ho the sun and the rain)

  He wrote and he wrote
  it was his way to grieve
(with a Hey ho the sun and the rain)
  The pleasure grief gave him
  you wouldn't believe
(Hey ho the sun and the rain)

  At length when the sorrow
  began to wear thin
(Hey ho the sun and the rain)
  He went out and brought
  a new torturess in
(Hey ho the sun and the rain)

  Turned out she loved him
  he found out too late
(Hey ho the sun and the rain)
  He's happy as hell
  but he cannot create
(Hey ho the sun and the rain)

Data

facts lie
behind the poems
which are true
fictions

My Rodney Poem

for Eddie Baugh;
& in memory of
Walter, 1942–1980

I

He lived
a simple life

He was a man
who cared
when anybody hurt
not just the wretched
of the earth

He dared
to be involved
in nurturing
upheavals

II

Frustrated by
the host of evils
he seemed to me a good
man reaching for the moon

He died
too soon

Windscreen

De garage people
seh de neat
crack in mi windscreen
bound to grow

an though it hardly showin
now, between vibration an de heat
it noh mus grow?

I climb inside
an measure. So I know:
de crack is growin.

Legion

And he asked him, What is thy name?
St Mark

1

in the agonising
calm

a self-
destructive dread

erupted
from the boneyard

howling

2

deadly bastard
fucking up
our lives

an intimate
disaster

littering the tombstones
with his shredded poems

3

dark dark dark
inside
the world i want
to bury

yerri mi mi nana
yerri mi...

Walk Good

Teck time
walk good

Yu buck yu foot
an memory ketch yu

like a springe